D1123109

Harvest of Light

Dedicated to Tzveka Halpern (1945–2001)
May his memory continue to bring light and blessing to the world . . .
And to the Halpern family from whom we learned to harvest olives.
— A.O.

To my family for enabling me to live my dreams:
My wife Nili and son Yagel. My parents Ze'ev (Z"L) and BatSheva;
Lauri, Rich, Amy, Cathy, Noah, Ethan, Billy, Elijah, Slick and Sanchez
. . . and of course, the Ofananskys!
— E.A.

PHOTO ACKNOWLEDGEMENTS

The hannukiah, oil jug, plate and bowl shown on pages 28–32 are the work of Tzfat potter Daniel Flatauer.
http://www.haaripottery.blogspot.com

Thanks to the staff at the Migdal olive press and their Association for the Benefit of the Child,
for allowing us to photograph the oil pressing process.

Text copyright © 2008 Allison Ofanansky
Photos copyright © 2008 by Eliyahu Alpern

Kar-Ben Publishing, Inc.
A division of Lerner Publishing Group, Inc.
241 First Avenue North
Minneapolis, MN 55401 U.S.A.
1-800-4-KARBEN

Website address: www.karben.com

Library of Congress Cataloging-in-Publication Data

Ofanansky, Allison.
    Harvest of light / by Allison Ofanansky ; illustrated by Eliyahu Alpern.
       p.   cm.
    Summary: An Israeli family raises olives and uses some of the oil to light their Hanukkah menorah.
    ISBN 978-0-8225-7389-0 (lib. bdg. : alk. paper)
    [1. Olive—Fiction. 2. Hanukkah—Fiction. 3. Israel—Fiction.] I. Alpern, Eliyahu, ill. II. Title.
PZ7.O31Har 2008
[E]—dc22   20070431330

Manufactured in the United States of America
1 2 3 4 5 6 – DP – 13 12 11 10 09 08

Harvest
of Light

By Allison Ofanansky
Photos by Eliyahu Alpern

KAR-BEN
PUBLISHING

At the beginning of spring, in the hills around the city of Safed, Israel, tiny white flowers blossom on the olive trees. When the days start to get hot, the flowers fall off and the first tiny green olives appear.

All summer long, I wait for them to ripen. This year I'm old enough to help with the harvest.

In the fall, before Sukkot, we pick the first green olives.

These will be to eat, not for pressing into oil. But olives right off the tree are bitter. They have to be pickled in salt water before they taste good.

We fill a basket with green olives. My Ima (that's my mom) cuts a small X into each one with a sharp knife, and I toss them into a bowl of cold water. Every day for a week, we drain the bowl and refill it with fresh water to wash away the bitter juice. At the end of the week, we pack the olives in glass jars with cloves of garlic, slices of lemon, spices, and salt water. The olives will soak for several months before they are ready to eat.

After Sukkot, the first rains fall. The olives turn from green to purple. We gather some of these darker olives for pickling. When my Ima cuts an X into them, drops of oil seep out.

As Hanukkah approaches, the olives start to turn black and shiny with oil. The branches sag from the heavy fruit. When it rains, some of the olives fall off the trees. It's time to harvest them for pressing into oil.

We wear old clothes because they'll get stained with oil. First, the grown-ups spread big, thick plastic sheets under one of the trees. With long, thin sticks, they shake and hit the branches. The olives rain down, pitter-patter. I help by pulling out all the little twigs and collecting the olives that have rolled off the tarp onto the ground.

I'm careful not to step on them.

Next Abba (that's my dad) climbs the tree. With a small saw, he prunes out some of the tangled branches. I help pull the olives off these branches.

When we're done, we move the tarps to another tree and fill another sack.

Some of the olives are all black. Some have swirls of purple and green. I put the prettiest ones in a little basket. I will use them to decorate around our Hanukkah menorah.

When I get restless, Abba gives me arithmetic problems to do with the olives. "Count ten into one pile," he says. "Now take away two. How many are left? Now add five olives. How many are in that pile?"

I love the olive trees. They are old and their branches twist into beautiful shapes. One tree has a seat just for me. When I get tired of helping, I climb up into it. From up high, I can see all around. The leaves on the grape vines and pomegranate trees have turned red and yellow.

A black and white woodpecker pecks a hole in the bark of another olive tree.

Across the valley, I hear voices and see small figures spreading a tarp under a tree. Our neighbors are collecting olives, too. Hanukkah is coming, and everyone needs oil.

All month, we collect olives. We move from tree to tree, filling big sacks. At the end of the day we dump them into a big pile. If we leave them in the sacks too long, they could get moldy. "How many olives are in that pile?" Abba asks, smiling. "I can't count them, there are too many!" I protest.

The pile of olives grows and grows. Now we have to take out the leaves so the oil won't be bitter.

We use a ramp covered with an old carpet. I help by pouring the olives down the ramp. The leaves stick to the carpet, and the olives roll into a tarp at the bottom. When all the olives are clean, we pour them back into their sacks. We load all the sacks and lots of empty jugs into a truck and drive to the olive press.

At the press, the olives are weighed and rinsed in water.

The clean olives are poured into a crusher where big stones crush them into a paste.

The paste is squirted onto mats.

The mats are stacked and rolled into a pressing machine where they are squeezed tightly. Oil still mixed with water drips out and is collected in a big tank.

The mixture is sucked into a centrifuge machine which whirls around very fast and separates the bitter water from the oil. The pure oil pours into a metal tub.

From there it is funneled into jugs to take home.

At dinner, Ima takes out the last bottle of old oil. That oil is clear and golden, unlike the new oil which is cloudy and green. She says new oil needs to settle for a few weeks before it is ready to use. But I want to taste the oil from olives I helped gather, so she mixes a few drops of it into the old oil. We dip fresh, warm pita bread into it. Delicious!

On the first night of Hanukkah, I arrange pretty olives around our menorah. Abba pours a little of the new oil into the glass cups. He reminds me it is the same kind of oil that was used to light the Temple menorah in Jerusalem long ago. When the Maccabees restored the Temple they found only enough oil to last for one day. But a miracle happened and it burned for eight days, enough time to harvest new olives and press them into oil.

After we sing the blessings, I hold Abba's hand as he lights a wick floating in the oil.

Then we sing Hanukkah songs and watch the flickering light of the burning oil—oil from olives I helped gather.